THE MISSIONS OF TEXAS

Janey Levy

PowerKiDS
press™

NEW YORK

Published in 2010 by The Rosen Publishing Group, Inc.
29 East 21st Street, New York, NY 10010

Book Design: Christopher Logan

Photo Credits: Cover (all images), pp. 3, 4, 6, 8, 12, 18, 23, 24, 26, 28, 30, 31, 32 (Texas emblem on all),
3–32 (textured background), back cover (Texas flag), p. 23 (mission) Shutterstock.com; p. 4 Hulton Archive/
Getty Images; pp. 5, 8, 10, 11, 16 (all images), 19 (cottonwood tree), 25, 29 (El Paso) Wikimedia Commons;
pp. 7 (map), 12 (maps) © GeoAtlas; p. 13 © Darlene Meader Riggs; p. 14 Peter Wilson/Getty Images; p. 15
Getty Images; p. 17 Jusepe de Ribera/Getty Images; p. 19 (Alamo) Panoramic Images/Getty Images; p. 21
Scenics of America/PhotoLink/Getty Images; p. 27 courtesy Library of Congress; p. 29 (cowboys and cattle)
SambaPhoto/Araquem Alcantara/Getty Images.

Library of Congress Cataloging-in-Publication Data

Levy, Janey.
  The Missions of Texas / Janey Levy.
     p. cm. — (Spotlight on Texas)
  Includes index.
  ISBN 978-1-61532-456-9 (pbk.)
  ISBN 978-1-61532-457-6 (6-pack)
  ISBN 978-1-61532-465-1 (library binding)
  1. Missions, Spanish—Texas—History—Juvenile literature. 2. Texas—History—To 1846—Juvenile literature.
  3. Franciscans—Missions—Texas—History—Juvenile literature. I. Title.
  F389.L48 2010
  976.4'01—dc22
                              2009042140

Manufactured in the United States of America

CPSIA Compliance Information: Batch # WW10RC: For further information contact Rosen Publishing, New York, New York at 1-800-237-9932.

CONTENTS

NEW ★ SPAIN

The year was 1519. The place was a huge area of North America called New Spain. Spanish **explorer** Alonso Álvarez de Pineda was mapping the coast of the Gulf of Mexico. Pineda and his men were the first Europeans to see the entire coast of what is today Texas. At the same time, **conquistador** Hernán Cortés was beginning the fight against Native Americans to **conquer** Mexico. Pineda and Cortés came to claim land for Spain and find riches. However, they didn't know much about this strange new land.

Many Native American tribes had lived for centuries in the place the Spanish called New Spain. The Spanish often fought the Native Americans to conquer them. Other times—mainly in **frontier** areas such as Texas—they tried to make Native Americans Spanish citizens using **missions**.

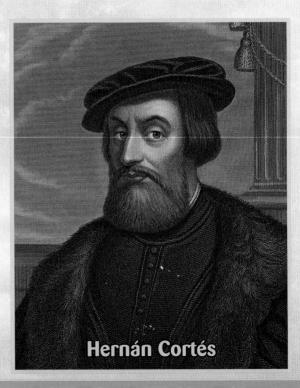

Hernán Cortés

This 1681 French map shows that Europeans still knew little about Texas long after the first explorers had arrived. The area that includes Texas is labeled "Terres Inconnues," or "Unknown Lands."

THE FRANCISCANS AND THEIR MISSIONS

Franciscans founded missions across Texas to teach Native Americans about Christian beliefs and practices. They also taught them Spanish laws and ways of life. The **missionaries** usually didn't force Native Americans to enter the missions. However, many came because the missions offered safety from enemies and a steady food supply. Those who came had to follow firm rules. The Franciscans hoped these Native Americans would finally become part of the society Spain was trying to build in New Spain.

The Franciscans

The Franciscans were an order, or group of monks and nuns, within the Catholic Church. St. Francis of Assisi founded the order in 1209. They believed they should stay poor so that worldly goods didn't become too important to them. At first, they spent their time preaching. Later, they took up educational and missionary work.

The Spanish built forts called presidios near the missions. Soldiers who guarded the missions lived in the presidios. Sometimes villas were built, too. These were ordinary towns not controlled by the Franciscans.

The Franciscans founded twenty-six missions in all. Most weren't as successful as the missionaries had hoped. However, they did much to shape modern Texas **culture**.

Spanish missions in Texas, 1659–1795

- ■ mission
- □ presidio

Dallas

El Paso

Austin ★

Houston

San Antonio

Corpus Christi

This map shows the locations of the Franciscan missions in Texas. Notice that most of them are in central, southern, and eastern Texas.

THE FIRST TEXAS MISSIONS

The Spanish didn't take much interest in Texas until long after 1519. In 1632, Franciscans built the first Texas mission, near the present city of San Angelo. The next missions were built in 1659 and 1680, near what is today El Paso. El Paso was also the location for the first Texas mission accompanied by a villa—Corpus Christi de la Isleta—which was built in 1682.

Corpus Christi de la Isleta

Left Events	Year	Right Events
Colony founded on Roanoke Island.	**1519**	Alonso Álvarez de Pineda maps coast of Texas. Hernán Cortés begins fight to conquer Mexico.
	1585	
Jamestown founded.	1607	
Plymouth Colony founded.	1620	Franciscans found first Texas mission near San Angelo.
New York founded.	1624	
	1632	
Maryland founded.	1634	
Connecticut becomes a colony.	1636	
Pennsylvania founded.	1643	
Rhode Island becomes a colony.	1647	
	1659	
New Jersey founded.	1660	Franciscans found second Texas mission near El Paso.
Carolina founded.	1663	
New Hampshire becomes a colony.	**1680**	Franciscans found third Texas mission near El Paso.
	1682	

The English Colonies

The United States didn't yet exist in the 1500s and 1600s. Along the Atlantic coast, however, England was founding colonies that would one day become free and form the United States. Use this timeline to compare events in Texas and along the Atlantic coast.

The Franciscans who founded Corpus Christi de la Isleta came from New Mexico. Angry Native Americans had driven them out of that area. They had forced Native Americans in New Mexico to work for them and banned ancient Native American practices. Finally, the Native Americans attacked the Franciscans and drove them away.

Not all Native Americans in New Mexico were angry with the Franciscans. Many Tigua Indians came with the Franciscans to El Paso and remained there.

The Lady in Blue

In the 1620s, some Native Americans in Texas and New Mexico claimed a lady in blue taught them Christian beliefs.

A Franciscan nun named María de Jesús de Agreda said she was the lady. However, María had never left Spain! How could she be the lady in blue? María said she was carried to this faraway land in dreams.

María de Jesús de Agreda

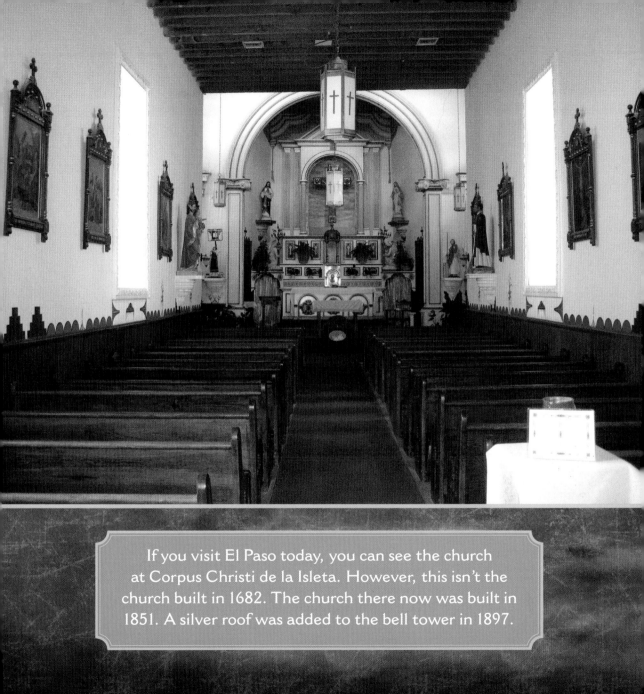

If you visit El Paso today, you can see the church at Corpus Christi de la Isleta. However, this isn't the church built in 1682. The church there now was built in 1851. A silver roof was added to the bell tower in 1897.

EAST TEXAS MISSIONS

The Spanish were very concerned with founding missions in east Texas. This was partly because they wanted to keep out the French. The French controlled neighboring Louisiana and wanted to spread their control into Texas. Alonso De León and Father Damián Massanet founded the first east Texas mission in 1690. They built it in the middle of a Hasinai (ha-SEE-ny) Indian settlement located on San Pedro Creek, near modern-day Augusta. The Spanish named the mission San Francisco de los Tejas.

East Texas

San Francisco de los Tejas mission ★

★Austin

San Antonio

Houston●

●Corpus Christi

Texas

The Franciscans at the mission quickly ran into problems. The Hasinais were interested in trading with the Franciscans. However, they weren't interested in the Franciscans' teachings. It was hard to get supplies to the mission since it was so far from Mexico. In 1693, the Franciscans burned the mission and returned to Mexico.

Texans consider the founding of San Francisco de los Tejas to be an important moment in state history. So in 1935 they established Mission Tejas Historical Park and built a log church to honor the original mission.

The Franciscans didn't give up plans for missions in east Texas. In 1716, they founded Nuestro Padre San Francisco de los Tejas near the earlier mission's location. Father Francisco Hidalgo was placed in charge.

In 1719, the Franciscans deserted this mission after the French attacked east Texas. However, they still didn't give up. They set up a mission nearby in 1721 and named it San Francisco de los Neches, after the Neche Indians.

East Texas has lands covered with water, like the area shown here. It also has many kinds of plants and animals. That's why Native Americans such as the Neche chose to live there.

Father Francisco Hidalgo

Francisco Hidalgo was born in Spain in 1659. He became a Franciscan when he was 15. In 1683, he traveled to New Spain. After several years in east Texas, he moved to the city of San Antonio in 1719. In 1725, his appeal to become a missionary to the Apaches of central and west Texas was refused. He withdrew to a mission in Mexico, where he died in 1726.

a Franciscan monk

This picture from around 1875 shows a Franciscan monk. Father Francisco Hidalgo and other Franciscans wore clothes like those shown here.

The Franciscans founded four more east Texas missions over the next few years. They weren't very successful. A few Native Americans accepted the Franciscans' teachings and joined Spanish society in New Spain. However, most were interested only in trade and help fighting their enemies.

East Texas Native Americans had strong societies of their own. Their farms and methods of trading provided almost everything they needed. They also didn't like the rules of mission life. The missions finally closed for good around 1730.

squash

corn

beans

The Three Sisters—squash, corn, and climbing beans—are the three main agricultural crops of many Native American groups in North America.

East Texas Missions

- San Francisco de los Tejas (1690–1693)
  - Nuestro Padre San Francisco de los Tejas (1716–1719)
    - San Francisco de los Neches (1721–1730)
- San José de los Nazonis (1716–1730)
  - Nuestra Señora de la Purísima Concepción (1716–1730)
- Nuestra Señora de Guadalupe (1716–1730)
  - Nuestra Señora de los Dolores de los Ais (1716–1730)

St. Francis of Assisi

St. Francis was born around 1182 to a wealthy family in Assisi, Italy. As a young man, he enjoyed fine clothes and food and having good times. A scary illness in 1204 made him realize this wasn't the best way to live. He decided he should remain poor and teach people about Christian beliefs. He founded the Franciscans in 1209. After he died in 1226, the Catholic Church made him a saint. Beginning in 1232, Franciscans gave great importance to education and spreading their ideas.

St. Francis of Assisi

THE ALAMO AND OTHER SAN ANTONIO MISSIONS

Have you heard of the Alamo? Many Americans know about the Battle of the Alamo, which was fought in 1836. However, did you know the Alamo was originally a mission called San Antonio de Valero? In 1718, Father Antonio de San Buenaventura y Olivares founded the mission west of San Pedro Springs in present-day San Antonio. He also founded the nearby San Antonio de Béxar Presidio and Villa de Béxar.

A powerful storm destroyed the mission in 1724. It was then moved to the east bank of the San Antonio River. It suffered Native American attacks during the 1730s and 1740s. In 1739, terrible sicknesses killed most Native Americans at the mission. The greatest number of Native Americans lived there during the 1750s. After that, the number dropped. In 1793, the Franciscans left the mission.

How did San Antonio de Valero Mission come to be called the Alamo? Spanish soldiers staying there in the early 1800s may have named it after the Mexican village they came from—El Alamo. Another possibility is that its name came from the cottonwood trees around it. The Spanish word for cottonwood is "alamo."

cottonwood tree

Alamo

In 1720, Father Antonio Margil de Jesús founded another San Antonio mission—San José y San Miguel de Aguayo. Like other missions, it was moved several times. Sicknesses killed most of San José's Native Americans in 1739. The mission's best years were in the late 1700s. It became famous for its beauty and strength. The central Spanish government took over control of the mission in 1794.

Three other important missions in San Antonio were first located in east Texas. They were moved to San Antonio in 1731 after the Franciscans gave up on the east Texas missions in 1730. Of these three, the most famous and successful was Nuestra Señora de la Purísima Concepción, which is often called Mission Concepción for short.

The church that now stands at San José was begun in 1768 and finished around 1777. It may seem rather plain today, but it was originally decorated with colorful patterns and many stone figures.

San José y San Miguel de Aguayo

Mission Concepción's church was built of **adobe**, then covered with stone and **plaster**. Paintings covered the plaster walls inside and outside the church. It was also decorated with carved figures. Mission Concepción was very successful in spreading Spanish culture during the 1750s, but its success didn't last.

The mission that began in east Texas as San Francisco de los Tejas became San Francisco de la Espada when it was set up in San Antonio. It's famous today for having the oldest continuously operating **irrigation** system in the United States.

The east Texas mission of San José de los Nazonis became San Juan Capistrano. It wasn't as successful as San Antonio's other missions. It suffered more Native American attacks because of its location. It didn't have enough land for its livestock and crops.

Unlike most of the old Spanish missions, Mission Concepción has never fallen apart, so it has never had to be put back together. It's just as it was when it was finished in 1755. If you visit it and look closely, you can see how buildings were put together in the mid-1700s!

Mission Concepción

La Bahía

"La Bahía" is Spanish for "the bay." The Spanish first used it as a short name for Matagorda Bay, which they called La Bahía del Espíritu Santo. A presidio founded there in 1721 had a long official name. However, it was usually called La Bahía. The following year, a mission was built nearby. It, too, was called La Bahía instead of its long official name.

The presidio and mission were twice moved farther inland, but they were still called La Bahía. Over time, a town grew up near them that was also called La Bahía. The town became important because many major roads crossed there. Although the mission lasted a long time, it wasn't considered successful. Few of the Native Americans who came there accepted the mission's teachings.

The Presidio La Bahía was moved to the Guadalupe River in 1726, then to the San Antonio River in 1747. The presidio built on the San Antonio River is still standing today and can be visited. The town that grew up around it is now called Goliad.

Presidio La Bahía

DEATH AT SANTA CRUZ DE SAN SABÁ

Since 1725, the Franciscans had wanted to found a mission for the Apaches. They finally took action in 1757. The governor of Texas warned against it. He said the Apaches only wanted a mission and presidio to guard them from their Comanche enemies. The Franciscans didn't listen. They founded a mission on the San Saba River near the modern town of Menard. They named it Santa Cruz de San Sabá.

The governor had been right. Comanches and other enemies of the Apaches burned the mission in 1758 and killed many inside. In 1759, Spanish soldiers fought and lost a battle with the Comanches and other attackers. With French guns and Spanish horses, the Native Americans had become a strong fighting force. They wanted to drive the Spanish off their land. Life in New Spain had changed forever.

This 1903 photo shows a group of Apaches on horseback. The Apaches came to Texas between about 1000 and 1400. They became known as great fighters. However, by around 1700, they were being forced to move by the more powerful Comanches.

The Last Texas Mission

By the late 1770s, the Spanish had decided missions weren't the best way to control New Spain. Few new missions were set up after that. The last mission was Nuestra Señora del Refugio. It was founded in 1793 near La Bahía del Espíritu Santo, at the modern town of Long Mott. Refugio suffered many problems. Fights often broke out between Native American groups there. Comanches and Karankawas regularly attacked. The mission finally closed in 1824.

Between 1824 and 1830, most remaining missions closed. The mission period ended when the missions around El Paso closed in 1852. In a few places, the missions had accomplished their purpose. However, most hadn't. The majority of Texas's Native Americans wanted to continue their old ways of life. They didn't want to become part of Spanish society in New Spain.

By the late 1700s, ranching and farming had become important to the way of life in Texas. The population in Texas was growing, and more and more people wanted to take over the missions' land so they could raise cattle and crops.

El Paso, 1886

cowboys and cattle

READER RESPONSE PROJECTS

- Use this book, the Internet, and other books to learn all you can about what the missions were like. Then draw a picture or create a model of a mission showing the different buildings you would find there and where they would be located.

- Choose one of the missions in this book or another mission you have heard of, and learn all you can about it. Then create a timeline for the mission on poster board. Add drawings or pictures to your timeline.

- Imagine that you are a Native American living in Texas during the mission period. Write a story telling about the missions, what they are like, what effect they have on your way of life, and how you feel about them. Share your story with your class or a friend.

GLOSSARY

adobe (uh-DOH-bee) Bricks or building matter made from sun-dried mud and straw.

conquer (KAHN-kuhr) To overcome by force of arms.

conquistador (kahn-KEES-tuh-dohr) A leader of the Spanish soldiers who conquered large parts of North and South America in the 1500s.

culture (KUHL-chur) The beliefs, arts, and way of life of a group of people.

explorer (ihk-SPLOHR-uhr) Someone who travels in search of new land.

Franciscan (fran-SIHS-kuhn) A monk or nun in the Catholic Church who belongs to the religious community founded by St. Francis of Assisi.

frontier (fruhn-TIHR) An area on the edges of settled territory.

irrigation (ihr-uh-GAY-shun) The use of man-made methods to supply water for crops.

mission (MIH-shun) A place where people work to spread their beliefs.

missionary (MIH-shuh-nehr-ee) Someone who serves at a mission.

plaster (PLAS-tuhr) A whitish mix of water, sand, and other matter that is used to cover walls.

INDEX